MW00884803

Sell Your Home with Feng Shui

A Complete Guide to Staging Homes for Quick Sale in Any Market

CHRISTINE AYRES & CINDY COVERDALE

AuthorHouse™
1663 Liberty Drive, Suite 200
Bloomington, IN 47403
www.authorhouse.com
Phone: 1-800-839-8640

AuthorHouse™ UK Ltd.
500 Avebury Boulevard
Central Milton Keynes, MK9 2BE
www.authorhouse.co.uk
Phone: 08001974150

© 2007 Christine Ayres & Cindy Coverdale. All rights reserved.

No part of this book may be reproduced, stored in a retrieval system, or transmitted by any means without the written permission of the author.

First published by AuthorHouse 5/2/2007

ISBN: 978-1-4259-7142-7 (sc)

Printed in the United States of America
Bloomington, Indiana

This book is printed on acid-free paper.

Bloomington, IN Milton Keynes, UK

authorHOUSE®

Library of Congress Control Number: 2006910342

With thanks to all our colleagues and friends
in the real estate community.

SELL YOUR HOME WITH FENG SHUI

Contents

SELL YOUR HOME WITH FENG SHUI

Introduction

Introduction

A New Tool For Selling Homes

Dealing with the ups and downs of the real estate market is an ongoing challenge for real estate professionals. What works one year may not be the best approach in the next. A seller's market can swiftly shift to a buyer's market and vice versa. Creative use of all available resources is the way to a consistently successful sales career. An exciting new tool for selling homes has been found in the ancient art of Feng Shui.

Real estate professionals across the country have come to appreciate the unique opportunity offered by preparing homes for the market with Feng Shui. You can join these successful salespeople by learning how to look at your listings in a new, Feng Shui way. Incorporating Feng Shui as a staging technique will give you an energetic edge in a very competitive marketplace. It is a great way to expand your staging expertise.

Staging real estate with Feng Shui can help expand a narrow market for a particular property and resolve inherent problems in the house that may have turned buyers away. Feng Shui enhancements can make a small living room look like a great room or transform a difficult entry into a beautiful, welcoming space. It can even help to sell an empty house.

You do not have to put in years of study or hire a professional Feng Shui consultant to put these simple and straightforward principles into practice. Using these techniques does not require a large financial outlay or a lot of time and effort. Often, simply shifting the placement of what is already present in the house can do the trick.

Sell Your Home With Feng Shui is intended for real estate professionals as well as homeowners who are preparing a house for sale. This information has been distilled from many years of experience in using Feng Shui enhancements to promote quick, easy real estate sales. Success stories are the norm, and "miracles" abound, no matter what the market, location, or history of a listing.

We all know the feeling of walking into a home and wanting to walk right back out. Using Feng Shui in your staging can change that feeling in any home to entice the buyer to want to stay and make an offer.

Want to be sold on this idea? Start using the information in the book with your listings and see what Feng Shui can do for you!

SELL YOUR HOME WITH FENG SHUI

Chapter 1

Chapter 1

WHAT IS FENG SHUI?

Feng Shui, pronounced "fung shway," is the ancient Chinese art of placement. It literally translates as "wind/water" and comes from an old poem that generally describes the ideal place to live as one where "the water is clear, the trees are lush, the wind is mild, and the sun is bright"—in other words, "location, location, location!"

Feng Shui has been making homes more welcoming and comfortable for thousands of years. It is a technique for uplifting and shifting the energy of a home. The overriding reason Feng Shui is alive and well around the world today is because it works and is easy to use. Using Feng Shui for real estate staging is a unique and specialized application of this ancient art.

The Feng Shui enhancements to a home for sale will be different from those for a seller staying in a house. The focus of this book is to provide techniques to attract the buyer, rather than making the home more comfortable for the seller. That is, the seller may have to shift a piece of furniture or relocate a favorite artwork in favor of a quick and profitable sale!

One tool you will use with your Feng Shui is the Bagua ("baa-gwa") energy map of a space. You will be using just a few key areas of this map when staging real estate with Feng Shui.

Ba means eight, and *gua* means area. The Bagua is an eight-sided map. It is said that this map was first written down in the year 888, and has survived simply because it is an accurate description of the way energy lays out in a space.

Looking at the Bagua drawing below, you will see three different entries, indicated with arrows coming into the space. These delineate three possibilities for the front door of the house.

REAL ESTATE BAGUA

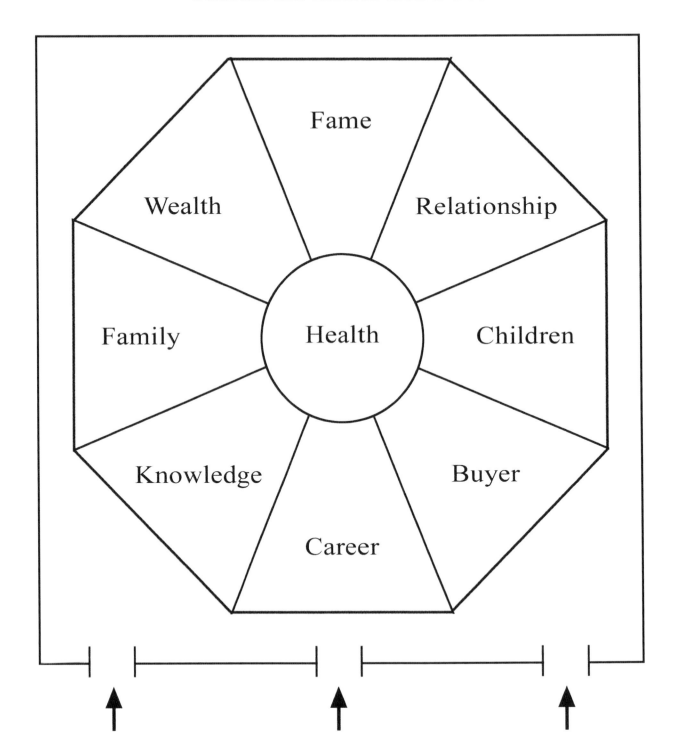

The door may come in on the left, center, or right as you look at the front of the house. This is where the house "inhales" its vitality, and it determines the energy layout for the rest of the house. Align the bottom of the Bagua with the front wall of the house, and you've got it!

The above Bagua has been especially modified for easy use in real estate sales. In this guide to staging with Feng Shui, you will be using the Career, Fame, Wealth, and Buyer areas. These are the spots in the house we want to be sure to enliven with light, color, or the placement of a few simple objects. For instance, the Career area is where your business cards should be placed. Hanging some wind chimes in the Buyer area will call in the buyer and fire up the showings. Some red flowers in the Fame area will increase the renown and reputation of your listing versus others. A water fountain or objects in specific colors can enliven the *chi* or energy of money.

So hold on to your Bagua and let's move on to the house itself.

SELL YOUR HOME WITH FENG SHUI

Chapter 2

Chapter 2

CREATE ENERGETIC CURB APPEAL

The very first impression, and the point at which the buyer starts making decisions about the property, is at the curb. Improving the curb appeal of a house gets us off on the right track and starts the buyer feeling positive about the property. It also inspires those drive-by "looky-loos" to want to take it a step further and come on in.

Clear the Path to a Sale

Is there a clear, inviting path to the front door? If not, trim back overgrown bushes or overhanging trees that obscure the path or block the view of the front door. It is essential to provide a clear path for *chi* flow up to the door.

You will often find, especially in older neighborhoods, that trees overwhelm the house. That is, they have grown so large that they tower over the roofline, block windows and entry paths, and visually diminish the house. This is the time to gently advise the seller to (a) trim away the lower branches of the trees to reveal the house, (b) thin out all the branches of the tree to allow more light and movement, or (c) remove the dominant trees and replace them with new, smaller specimens.

A beautiful path welcomes the buyer to this house.

Overgrown landscape overwhelms this house and makes it difficult to locate.

A house for sale in an older neighborhood had 20-30 year old trees and shrubs that had grown so large that they obscured the front of the house and towered over the roof line. The comments that came from prospective buyers, over months on the market, all had the same theme: the house is too small. Indeed, it was not the biggest house on the block, but the first impression created by the dominating landscape was very hard to overcome.

The house needed to reclaim its charm and stature. First, the evergreens were trimmed up so that the front of the house and the windows could be seen from the street. Then, deciduous trees were thinned considerably so that the roof was more visible. Overgrown shrubs were completely removed around the base of the house, replaced by flowers, which had the additional effect of letting more light into the house through the windows. A weathervane was installed on the peak of the roof. It was also suggested that the house be painted a lighter color to give it bigger profile.

This was a more extensive exterior staging, but paid off with a new perception by buyers of a charming, tree-shaded cottage that brought a quick offer from a retired couple.

Cracked concrete or broken stepping stones on the path to the house send an immediate negative message about maintenance and upkeep. Repair these "first steps" to a sale to bring the buyer in with a fresh first impression.

Depending on the parking situation at the property, it can also be a plus to put in a stepping-stone path directly from the street to the door. This is especially useful if the only approach to the front door is from the driveway, and one would be crossing a lawn or other planted area to go directly to the front door from the street. It also helps to pull the *chi*, or energy, up from the street to the house.

Locate the House

House numbers are important to give the buyer a sense of arrival and welcome at the property. Don't rely on "There's a For Sale sign in front." This is not enough to assure the buyer that they have located the right property. You want the house to be very easy to find.

Make sure that the house numbers are large and readable, and that they contrast with the background they are placed on. For example, brown numbers on a brown house are useless. Red, black, or gold are great colors to use, depending on the background. Numbers should be clearly readable from the street. They belong out on the front of the house or garage, not hidden under a shady porch overhang.

Another place to insure there are clear house numbers is on the mailbox at the street. Replace numbers if they are chipped, faded, or missing. It is also a good idea to repaint or replace an old mailbox. It gives a great first impression and updates the house.

Painting the trim is another way to make the house pop and look fresh. Lighter colors of trim can make a small house appear larger.

Lift the Chi

A house that sits below grade, or street level, needs some Feng Shui enhancement. When you look down at a doorway, it lowers your *chi* or energy. Just as when you drop your chin when you are sad, you lift your chin up when feeling great. The purpose here is to lift the gaze of the buyer by putting something eye-catching up higher. When you stand at street level you should look straight across and up a bit at the house numbers, a Welcome plaque, or decoration on the outside of the house.

Light fixtures can also do the trick, provided they are raised to the proper position. These eye-catchers should be placed above the garage doors or above the front door to be most effective.

Painting the trim around the roof a light, bright color will also give a below-grade house an energetic lift up to eye level.

Bright trim raises the eye on this below grade house.

Convert Problem Stairs into a Plus

Houses with substantial outside stairs make more work and create a problem for the buyer. You want to make the approach as easy as possible, so these types of stairs need attention. If there is an intermediate landing, this is a great place to have the buyer pause. Place a small bench on the landing, ensuring that it does not actually block the walking area of the stairs. Even a pot of colorful flowers will catch the eye and create the "pause" feeling.

You can use welcoming statuary, such as waving bears and the like, to bring the welcome forward to greet the buyer. The concept here is to avoid the "work, work, work, and then we get to the front door" experience. Give the buyer something pleasant on the way up as a reward for the climb, and the climb will seem shorter.

Bring the welcome even closer by framing the base of the stairway with a Welcome mat at the bottom and a pair of potted trees or containers of flowers on either side.

Success Story

A beautifully maintained, newer home had been on the market for several months during the strong spring selling season and required staging. The one comment that came up repeatedly with prospective buyers was that there were too many outside stairs. This was also discouraging drive-by lookers and those seeing promotional photos. These were, indeed, formidable stairs with two landings before you arrived at the front door.

First, the window boxes on the front of the house and top of the stairs were filled with bright red flowers. Then, a round pot of the same flowers was placed on the first landing. On the second landing, a small bench was added. An ornamental, metal rooster was attached to the railing here—a motif that was already on the window shutters above. Two more pots of red flowers were set to frame the base of the stairs and a Welcome sign was staked into one of the pots, facing the street.

The arduous climb to the front door was transformed into a beautiful enhancement to curb appeal. Multiple offers were received and there were no more comments about too many stairs.

Staggered flower pots break up the climb to the front door.

Generate Sales with Great Front Doors

The front door is the "mouth of chi" for the house—it is where the home inhales its vitality. This is a very important factor in curb appeal, so it deserves some attention.

Front doors should contrast with the surrounding façade of the house so that they "pop" and create a strong entry to pull in the buyer. When the door is the same color as the house or trim, *chi* just bounces right off. The door needs to be a dramatic entrance to the property.

A new coat of paint or stain will freshen up any door and make a great first impression. The same is true of door hardware. If it is scratched or weatherworn, replace it with a new set when the door is redone. This is another way to avoid sending any signals about deferred maintenance to the buyer.

A Welcome mat as wide as the door is a must. A postage stamp-size doormat diminishes the entry. If you have a double-door entry to deal with, then use a double-size mat, even when only one side will be opening. You want to emphasize this mouth of *chi* and make it as large as possible. A black mat, with or without "Welcome" on it, will work nicely. Don't skimp here! Spend a little to make the best first impression. You can recycle these mats to the next house.

As mentioned above in the Stairs section, frame the doorway with matching pots of red flowers or evergreen trees on both sides. This will expand the entry even more and send out the "Welcome" signals to the buyer.

If there is a wide front porch and you will not block the path to the door, then certainly add a welcoming bench here. It will be the first open-arms welcome to the buyer and says "There is a place for you here."

Occasionally you may find that the front door is not on the front façade of the house, but down the side of the house and out of sight. This hidden door makes it difficult for a buyer to feel a sense of arrival. In this case, there is no immediate welcome for the buyer and they must work harder to get into the house.

The bright contrasting color of this doors catches the eye and pulls in the buyer.

Success Story

There is a housing development in which a number of properties have been staged for sale, where almost all of the homes have a hidden door located on the side of the house. Inevitably, these are the homes that do not get traffic and sit stagnant when put on the market. In each and every case, after staging with Feng Shui was completed, the showings picked up and the houses sold.

Here are some suggestions for staging a house with a hidden door:

- Place a welcome bench out front that is visible from the street.

- Have large, readable house numbers on the front of the house and mailbox.

- Clear the path back to the front door of all intruding bushes or trees.

- Line the path going back to the front door with bright flowers or lights.

- Hang a wind chime outside on the Buyer corner of the house.

- Paint the hidden front door red or other bright, contrasting color.

- Frame the door with pots of bright flowers.

- Place a Welcome mat and Welcome sign at the door.

- Make sure the promo photos include a shot of the front door.

One last note regarding front doors: be sure that the door opens easily and does not squeak, stick, or make noise as it opens. A little WD40 can go a long way to let the energy, and the buyer, enter effortlessly and without distraction.

Where to Place Signage

The best place for your sign is in the Buyer corner of the front yard. As you stand in the driveway, this is the near right corner of the property. This will help to call in the buyer. Remember that the Buyer *gua* is not just the corner, but an entire area (see Bagua map), so there is some flexibility here. Note: a sign at right angles to the street will capture more *chi* and activity than one set flat and parallel to the house.

For Sale sign placed properly in the near right corner of the property.

SELL YOUR HOME WITH FENG SHUI

Chapter 3

Chapter 3

WELCOME THE BUYER

As the buyer enters the home, the entry must welcome and provide a space to pause and arrive—literally and energetically—before stepping into the first room.

Enlarge the Entry

Make the entry/foyer space feel as large as possible by having the front door open toward the largest part of the area. It is also important to have the directional flow of the entry go toward the "room of first impression" described in the next chapter.

Move any object that blocks the entry. This might be a bench, coat rack, or too-large entry table. Think of it in these terms: If a tall person were to fall flat on the floor at the doorstep, his head should not hit anything!

For furniture here, a small table for your business cards to rest upon is a good idea. A half-circle table is ideal, as it is easier to move past its rounded curve. The best container for the business cards is a metal bowl or plate. Second choice is a holder of any material that is black or silver in color.

Brighter is also better. Good lighting is important in the entry. It lifts the energy and is much more welcoming than a dark, small space. You can add a light or, if feasible, just increase the wattage in existing fixtures. A large mirror in this room can also reflect more light into the area.

Entry table with career enhancements and artwork depicting selling point of a house.

Reinforce Selling Points

The first piece of art encountered upon entry is very important, as it can set the tone for the entire house. Are you emphasizing the location of the property—golf course, ski lodge, mountains, lake, near an important landmark—as a selling point? If so, this first piece of art or photo should reflect the setting. Is it a cabin, cottage, villa, or penthouse? Again, make sure the initial art or photo works to reinforce this presentation. Often, the seller already has this piece somewhere in the house. Move it to the entry area to support your strong selling point.

If the property is especially large or historically significant, giving it a name will provide a special status and sense of place to the listing. Signage with this name, or artwork depicting the theme, can be placed in the entry.

Success Story

Many of our clients live in homes with a view of beautiful Lake Tahoe. Some of these views can only be characterized as a "peek" of the lake, but this can often be enhanced with Feng Shui staging techniques. One home in particular had a view only from one room, but was being marketed as a view home. The room with the view was the chosen room of first impression, the room the buyer should encounter first.

A runner rug was placed in the hall, leading directly to the room with a view. Then, a mirror was moved to hang directly across from the window with the view. This reflected in and doubled the view in the room. Patio furniture was arranged on the deck, with a clear path to the sliding doors, created by moving blocking furniture aside. This invited buyers to easily step out and enjoy the advertised view. Then, photographs and artwork of the view, in this case Lake Tahoe, were placed in the master suite and throughout the house. Thus, the selling point of a house with a view was strongly reinforced. The seller received an offer that week and moved on to a house with an even greater view.

Solve the Ups and Downs of an Entry Staircase

If the property has a set of stairs going up *and* a set of stairs going down off the entry, these need to be addressed. You want to lead the buyer to the best room to see first. Therefore, you need to emphasize the preferred set of stairs and downplay the other.

Place a small rug at the base of the "good" stairs. Draw the eye in this direction by placing a large or bright piece of artwork at the base of this stairwell's wall.

One last point: Make sure this direction is also well-lit. Downplay the other direction and leave it without decoration.

SELL YOUR HOME WITH FENG SHUI

Chapter 4

Chapter 4

Use the Room of First Impression to Sell the House

This is the room that sells the house. The first room the buyer steps into is the one in which they decide whether or not they like the house. This may be a very conscious "aha" experience, or a more subtle, unconscious acceptance. Every other room in the house will confirm this initial impression. The room of first impression is the most important room in using Feng Shui for staging.

Select the Best Room

If the view is one of the biggest selling points for this property, then select the room with the best view. Make sure that the buyer can walk unobstructed right to the view window or out to the deck or balcony. Thus the buyer gets instant fulfillment for what they came to see: the view.

You can reflect the view into the house by using a mirror, or art framed in reflective glass, on the wall opposite the view. This way, the view becomes more omnipresent. When the buyer turns away from the window, the view is still there reflected on the opposite wall. Do this not only in the room of first impression, but throughout the house wherever possible.

When your promotional material for a property emphasizes the great room, gourmet kitchen, or family game room, then this will be the best room of first impression. When selling points are easily seen and readily accessible, the buyer's expectations will be satisfied and they will immediately feel at home.

Direct the Buyer to the Best Room

You want to lead the buyer to the room of your choice. If the entry/foyer opens equally to two different spaces—for example, a living room and a kitchen, or a family room and a living room—then you must direct the buyer to the best room of first impression. This can be done in a number of ways, depending on how the space presents itself.

A runner rug leading the buyer to the best room of first impression is an obvious choice. Another technique is to move a dramatic piece of art or sculpture to pull the eye of the buyer in the intended direction while downplaying the less desirable direction.

Front doors that open in the way we wish to direct the buyer are perfect. If the existing door does not do this, consider flipping the door or installing a new one. The most important factor is getting the buyer into your choice of room of first impression as easily and effortlessly as possible.

Set Up Welcoming Furniture

When the buyer moves from the entry to the room of first impression, they should have a clear path. That is, the buyer has a direct path into the room without having to walk around a chair, table, or other obstacle.

Place a large chair, couch, or loveseat directly opposite and facing the entry path into this room. It gives an open-arms welcome to the buyer, and says "Come on in, there's a place for you here!"

Walking into the back of a couch will simply bounce the chi, and the buyer, right back out of the house. Walking into a welcoming furniture arrangement will give the buyer the feeling that they are home.

It is very important to remember that we are dealing with form over function in staging real estate with Feng Shui. The primary concern is the *impression* the room gives, not its actual functionality for the seller. For example, the seller's favorite TV chair may have to be shifted in the interest of creating a welcoming effect for the buyer.

A runner rug directs the buyer to the selected room of first impression.

Open Up Small Areas

You also want to arrange the furniture to make the room appear as large as possible. Open up small, cozy areas that may have served the seller, but now tend to break up a large room into small spaces. Where there might have been two seating areas, create one large open space.

Avoid using area rugs, as they also tend to break up larger spaces into smaller ones. Fewer, larger pieces of art are preferable to numerous small ones to make walls appear spacious.

Many times this room simply has too much furniture in it. Thin out the extraneous pieces and store or move them to other rooms. Remember, you are not selling furniture here, you are selling the house. Often rooms can look like beautiful furniture showrooms, but you cannot appreciate the size of the room. In some cases, the furnishings actually detract from the view or other important selling points.

Make sure that valances do not cover windows. Move them up above the glass to give the appearance of larger windows. Good light, natural and artificial, makes a room feel bigger. Uplighting with sconces or torchiere lights can lift low ceilings and expand dark corners.

Use Inviting Color

Color will lift the *chi* of the room and make it more lively and inviting. If the room is done in neutral colors, add bright pillows on couches and chairs and choose lighter and brighter artwork.

Painting an accent wall in the room of first impression can give it a nice dimension. If the room lacks windows or just feels like a box, then an accent wall can open it up. The best wall to paint is the one directly across from the entrance. A bolder shade of the existing wall color can be used, or emphasize a color that is already present in furniture or art.

If the walls and ceiling are the same color, either (1) paint the ceiling lighter than the wall, or (2) paint the wall a deeper, bolder color than the ceiling. The contrast between the wall and ceiling will create the effect of lifting the ceiling, creating more circulation in the room and making the room feel larger.

This living room welcomes the buyer with open arms.

This furniture placement bounces the buyer out of the room.

SELL YOUR HOME WITH FENG SHUI

Chapter 5

Chapter 5

PREPARE THE MASTER BEDROOM– THE BUYER'S ROOM

The master bedroom is next in importance in staging real estate with Feng Shui. This is the room of the person who writes the check—the buyer. Whether this is a single person or a couple, this room needs to appeal to the buyer.

Create Pleasing Proportion

The master bedroom will not show properly if the furniture is not in proportion to the room. What size is the existing bed in this room? If it is a King and it fits well in the space, great. If it is a King and you can barely enter or walk around the room, then it's time to make a change.

Using a Queen bed to allow for matching bedside tables, furniture that does not block windows, and an easier entry into the room is a much better choice in a cramped master bedroom. All the furniture must look as if it fits in the room. If not, the room appears smaller.

Expand the Space

This room needs to have good circulation and look as large as possible. The buyer will feel the room is larger when the furniture is in proportion to the room. The best décor in the world will not sell this room to the buyer if it overwhelms the space.

Set the head of the bed against one of the far walls—the walls that are farthest from the door to the master bedroom. This makes the room feel bigger, as you don't have to walk around the bed to enter the room. Painting the bed wall will also give a boxy room dimension and draw the eye, and the buyer, into the room.

Often simply thinning out extra chests of drawers or chairs in the room will help to open up the space. Move the linen chest or loveseat at the end of the bed out of the room. Create a clear pathway to windows or attached bathrooms.

The Bedroom is a Bedroom

You want this room to give a warm welcome to the buyer. Make sure it shows as a bedroom, not a bedroom/office or bedroom/workout space; do not confuse or clutter the energy in the master bedroom with extraneous purposes. You are telling the buyer that the house is too small or inadequate when you represent this room as anything but the master bedroom. Exercise equipment should be only in a designated exercise room or removed from sight. Desks and office equipment should be only in dens or offices.

A bright accent wall pulls the buyer into the master bedroom.

SELL YOUR HOME WITH FENG SHUI

Chapter 6

Chapter 6

ENHANCE THE BAGUA AREAS

Now we come to the more energetic or transcendental Feng Shui enhancements. These relate directly to you, the real estate professional. The sale of the property has a direct effect on your career, your fame and reputation, and your wealth. Let's look again at the Bagua energy map of the home.

Activate Career

Front and center in the Bagua is the Career area, the front and center of the home. This is the place to make enhancements to activate your career energy. We recommend that you set a small metal bowl or dish holding your business cards here. In most homes, this turns out to be near the front door. The bowl can be placed on a small entry table or on the first piece of furniture encountered in the room of first impression.

The Career *gua*, or area, is also where a water element can really get things moving. A small desktop fountain, bubbling away, can welcome the buyer and get the *chi* for the sale of the home moving. Be sure, though, that the direction of the water flow is *into* the house, not toward the door. You want to bring money, luck, and the buyer in, not push them out.

Water can be brought to this area symbolically if a water fountain is not feasible. Pictures of water (seascapes, lakes) or water animals (fish, frogs, water birds) can be used. Choose a dish for your business cards made of metal (metal produces water in Feng Shui), or one that is colored silver, black, or deep blue.

REAL ESTATE BAGUA

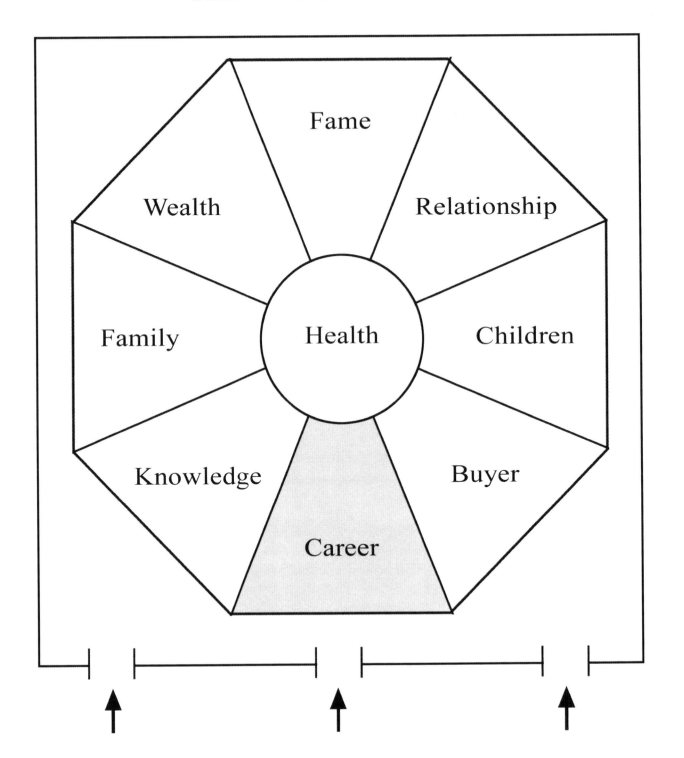

The water element enhances career energy.

Call in the Buyer

This area is where you can enliven the energy of buyers and call them to the house. The location of the buyer's energy is the front right area of the property, inside the house and out.

Hang a wind chime with hollow metal tubes under the eaves of the house outside or inside the corner of this room in the right front. It may even be the garage. In whatever room this area falls, we want to pay it some Feng Shui attention. Another outside enhancement for this corner can be a flag. This is especially useful for cul-de-sac homes—it keeps the *chi* moving in an otherwise stagnant situation.

This is also your first choice for sign placement. As you face the front of the house, the front right corner of the lot is the best place for your sign. At a right angle to the street is best. If CCRs limit you to a sign attached to the house, then the front right corner of the house is the place for the sign. This charges up the energy for a sale.

If a particular property keeps falling out of escrow, then you want to "ground" the energy here with some weight. Move the heavy armoire or bookcase to this area. Even a symbolic decorative bowl of river stones or a plant in a large pot will help. Heavy statuary or boulders outside off this corner of the house will help to hold the buyer's energy.

These weighty outdoor enhancements should also be used if the Buyer area of the house is missing. Place them in the spot where the two walls of the house would meet if you were squaring up the house. Plant a tree at this juncture. (Important: No downward-drooping or weeping trees!)

REAL ESTATE BAGUA

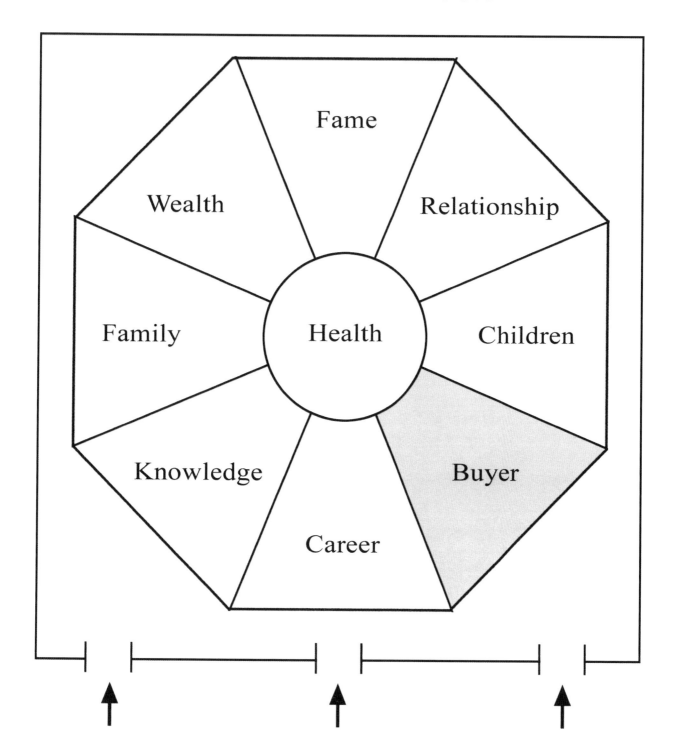

Wind chimes call in the buyer.

The boulder completes the missing Buyer area of this house.

Fire Up Fame and Reputation

Making a sale will be a feather in your cap and a boon to your reputation. A Feng Shui enhancement in the Fame area of the house will help this along. The Fame area is the center rear of the house. If there is a fireplace, fire pit, or stove here, this is a great head start on a fire element. Outside, move the barbeque grill to the center rear of the house.

No matter what room is in the Fame *gua*, you can add some fire to it by placing something red here. For example, in a kitchen you could use a bowl of red apples or a string of red chili peppers. In a bathroom, a nice red candle (it does not have to be burning) will light up your fame and that of the house. A vase of red flowers can be placed almost anywhere as well.

In regard to fireplaces, be sure that any fireplace is "fed." That is, do not leave a gaping, empty fireplace box. Lay in kindling and logs, as if you are ready to throw a match on. As an option, you can use something decorative such as white birch logs or pine cones. This energetic opening to the house must be filled. So, feed the fire!

REAL ESTATE BAGUA

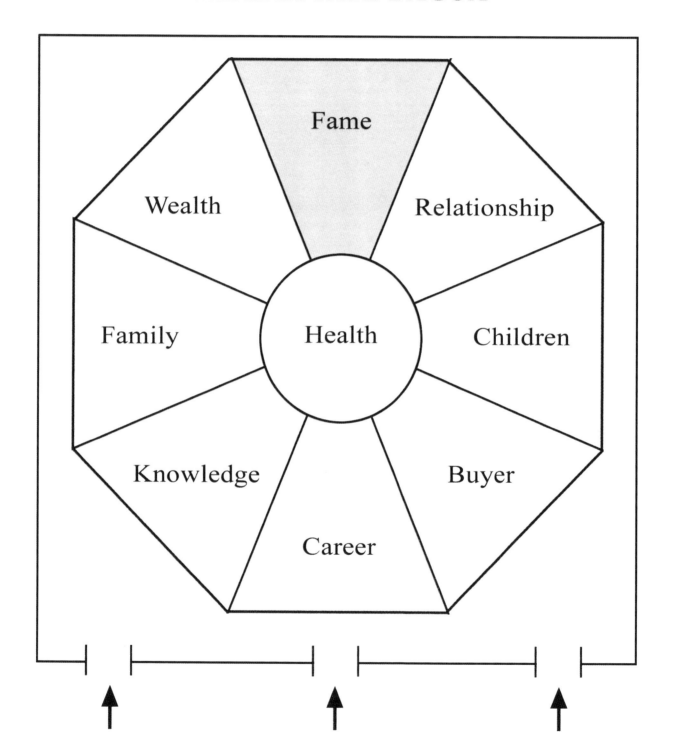

Red flowers enliven the fame of the house and that of the real estate professional.

Generate Wealth and Abundance

This life area of the Bagua will be a plus for the real estate professional and the seller. The Wealth area is the far left corner of the house. There are many ways to generate energy with Feng Shui in this area.

Several colors serve to enhance Wealth and Abundance. Anything with purple, red, green, gold, or silver placed in this *gua* will give it a lift. This can be a decorative object, linens, furniture, art, or any item that suggests the good life. Think "abundance" and choose an object that embodies this concept, like an expensive silver candlestick, original artwork, or amethyst crystal.

Metal chimes are good Feng Shui additions here. An upward-growing, as opposed to weeping, plant or tree provides great energy, too. The water elements described in the Career section, such as fountains and water pictures, also work wonders for Wealth and Abundance.

Use Universal Feng Shui Enhancements

What if you just can't fill the bill when it comes to finding the objects you need to enhance the Bagua areas? There are two universal Feng Shui enhancements you can use in all three of these *gua*s:

A round, faceted crystal can be hung in the Buyer corner, the Wealth corner, or the center of the Fame area. This crystal prism is a traditional Feng Shui enhancement for uplifting *chi*. It reflects light and creates movement. It can be hung by a red string or a more discreet piece of fishing line. The best lengths for the string are either three, six, nine, or twelve inches, depending upon the height of the ceiling. It's best to hang them high, up out of the way.

The second enhancement is one that is seen more frequently these days, and that is bamboo. A pot of "lucky bamboo" is another universal way to lift energy in any area. Bamboo is hollow, and the concept is that it brings up the *chi* of the earth through its stalk. Nine pieces of bamboo in a pot is ideal, although the presence and placement of any bamboo is a plus.

REAL ESTATE BAGUA

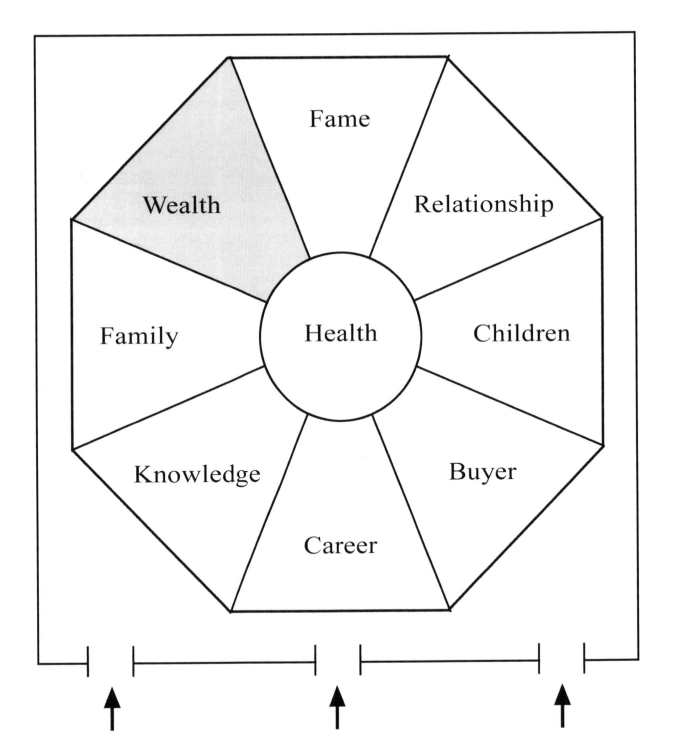

A round faceted crystal will uplift and expand energy.

Bamboo is an enhancement that can be used almost anywhere.

SELL YOUR HOME WITH FENG SHUI

Chapter 7

Chapter 7

TIPS TO BROADEN THE MARKET

You want your listing to appeal to as many people as possible, without presenting a property so neutral that it has no appeal whatsoever. The goal in using Feng Shui to stage real estate is to remove as many limitations as possible so that we have a large pool of buyers.

Clear the Clutter

Clutter is dead energy. It manifests as stacks of stagnant *chi* on the floor, in the hallways, on the shelves, in the closets. Removing this stagnation enlivens the entire house and increases energetic circulation throughout. You can turn a dead listing into a live one by clearing the clutter.

A good place to start is on the floor. Clear hallways, walkways, and staircases so that it is easy to move from room to room and floor to floor. This will get things moving and make the next step easier. Second, remove as many objects as possible from tabletops and counters. This will allow light to reflect off these surfaces, the rooms to feel brighter and bigger, and energy to flow more freely throughout the house.

You can cut down on the appearance of clutter by thinning out objects sitting on open shelves. Cover open shelving by installing doors or hanging fabric over it. This includes the garage storage shelves. Every little visual object has *chi* and can create chaos in the space. If the buyer feels overwhelmed or distracted by all the clutter, they will not make an offer.

Clutter also gives the impression of dirt and neglect. It will send the buyer a message that the house needs maintenance or repair, even if this is not the case. Encourage the seller to start moving by packing up the clutter and minimizing the "stuff" in the house.

Thin Out Personal Items

One person's clutter is another person's treasure. Convincing the seller that their personal collection of porcelain pigs is not a selling point goes a long way in depersonalizing the house. One little welcome bear on the doorstep is better than a home stuffed with bears on every surface. Collections are simply too much of a good thing; they take up space and divert the eye from the selling points of the house.

If the home is filled with personal items, it makes it more difficult for the buyer to envision themselves living there. It is as if they have to force their way in, from an energetic standpoint.

Take down all family photos, kids' art, school certificates, golf trophies, whatever may have a family name or face on it. This includes family name signs on the house, such as "The Smiths."

This is another box for the seller to pack now: personal items.

Success Story

A classic example of too much of a good thing was found in a listing that was stuck on the market. On arriving to stage the house with Feng Shui we were greeted, and greeted, and greeted--with bears! There were bears on the Welcome mat, bears on the walls, bears on the kitchen and bathroom towels, carved bears and porcelain bears everywhere. You get the picture. When asked, "What is going on with the bears?" The seller answered, "What bears?"

It can happen that sellers are so used to their collections, decorating themes, or accumulated clutter that they actually are no longer aware of it. After a tearful discussion of packing away the bear figurines and suggestions to replace bear artwork with landscapes, bear towels with solid colors, the seller understood that her house was repelling buyers that did not share her passion for her furry friends. She began packing boxes, which soon went in the moving van as the house closed in a month.

Remove Offensive Items

We all know there is no accounting for taste. To avoid offending a buyer, it is best that questionable items go into that first wave of packing boxes. Any item of a distinctly religious nature (e.g., Buddhas, crucifixes, menorahs) should be put away. Dead animal heads or bodies are a definite no-no. The same goes for firearms. These should be removed from sight. Again, remind the seller that we are appealing to as many buyers as possible.

It also helps to pack away anything of a political nature, even if it's a photo of the seller shaking the President's hand. It may be a source of pride to the seller, but offensive to the buyer.

Nudes also fall into this category, even if your seller feels that they are done in the most tasteful manner possible. This includes any depiction of a partially or completely nude human body. We are appealing to all ages and sensibilities here, and nothing should risk putting the buyer off.

SELL YOUR HOME WITH FENG SHUI

Chapter 8

Chapter 8

Solve Common Problems

When staging real estate with Feng Shui, you can solve problems with listings that otherwise might be difficult to overcome. This is because Feng Shui works with the energy of the property and qualities that might not be as tangible, and therefore harder to shift.

Rehabilitate a Bad Reputation

If it is known that someone has passed away in this home, or that there has repeatedly been serious illness, divorce, bankruptcy, or other misfortune at this property, it may be an obstacle to a sale. There are two ways to address this situation:

First, work on the Fame and Reputation area. Move the barbeque grill to the center rear wall behind the house. This brings the needed fire element to the Fame area. Tiki torches or a fire pit will work, too. Hang a wind chime under the eaves of the house at the center rear, to lift reputation. Inside, use red candles (no need to light them) or a bouquet of fresh or silk red flowers near the center rear wall of the home to rehabilitate a bad reputation.

Second, create a new, pleasant-sounding name for the property and mount a sign near the door: Water's Edge, Eagle's Roost, Quail Run, Oak Hill, whatever suits the property. Give it a new identity and new energy, even if it's just on the listing sheet and Internet posting.

Note: If the negativity is very strong, call in a Feng Shui consultant to do a space clearing in the home. Using a few simple tools, a professional Feng Shui consultant can give the house a blessing and clearing to remove any residual negative *chi* and give the house a fresh start.

Falling Out of Escrow—Reverse the Pattern

If a particular property keeps falling out of escrow, there is obviously a pattern here. You want to hold on to the buyer and not let the contract slip away. Many times you will find that the Buyer's *gua* is a bathroom or other draining space. Even if it is not, there are Feng Shui cures to hold this energy together.

Place a heavy piece of furniture in the Buyer's corner. (Reminder: this is the near right corner of the house as a whole.) Depending upon which room this is, you could use a heavy bookcase, large armoire, big couch or chair, or other substantial piece of furniture. This will help to ground the Buyer energy. If it is in the garage, stack up packed boxes. Place heavy statuary or boulders outside off this corner of the house as well.

If the Buyer area does happen to be a bathroom, then we need to get earthy! In the cycle of the elements, earth obstructs water—think of a dam holding water back. So our Feng Shui enhancement here is earth: earth-tone towels, wall color, ceramics, accessories. It is not the place for more water such as seashells, lighthouses, boats or fish. Add a decorative ceramic or glass dish with nice rounded river stones or a large piece of quartz crystal. Keep the toilet seat down and all drains closed and covered. You want to hold the buyer's *chi* in and not let it go down the drain.

Adjust Adjacent Property Chi

"Location, location, location" is a real estate mantra. Staging real estate with Feng Shui cannot change the neighborhood, but it can mitigate negative effects.

If your listing is the smallest property on the block and is overshadowed by tall buildings, either residential or commercial, then some Feng Shui to adjust the energy is in order. Install a weathervane on the highest roof peak to lift the *chi* of the property. And this is another instance when painting the trim a light color can lift the presence of the house.

If the neighbors have old appliances in the front yard or have created other less-than-uplifting views, there are two solutions. One is to create a foreground screen for the buyer. For example, if the undesirable view is out the kitchen window, then hang a decorative piece of stained glass in the window or place a colorful plant in front of it. The idea is to give the eye a foreground to look at, rather than let it be pulled out to the undesirable view.

A weathervane helps this house to hold its own against a dominant neighbor.

The same can be accomplished with a bit of intentional landscape screening, by planting shrubs and trees between the house and the offending view. Even a birdbath or birdfeeder will bring uplifting *chi* to the yard and divert the eye. The seller can also install top-down-bottom-up blinds on the window to block the offending view and yet allow light to filter through.

The second solution is a Bagua Mirror cure. A Bagua Mirror is a Feng Shui tool for pushing away energy that does not belong to you and that you do not wish to accept. It is a small round mirror, traditionally set in an octagonal wooden frame.

Place the mirror facing the view you wish to diminish. This can be in a window facing outward, behind draperies or artwork, or even outside up under the eaves. We have had great success with buyers walking right past the offending view, where previously they had paused to comment.

Success Story

Using a Bagua Mirror can have immediate and surprising results. A very desirable house was listed in a fast-moving market. Showings were frequent, however no offers were coming in. In the entry foyer was a large window that framed a view of the neighbor's yard—full of dismantled cars and motorcycles. This was creating a very negative first impression with prospective buyers, even though many expressed they "loved" the house.

Feng Shui enhancements were suggested to lessen the impact of the foyer view. A Bagua Mirror was hung in the window, facing the offending view. Then, top-down / bottom-up blinds were installed in this window. When the blinds were pulled up from the bottom, a view of the sky was visible from the top half of the window and the view of the neighbor's yard was blocked. A very dramatic piece of art was moved so that it hung directly across from the entry, thus catching the eye of the buyer and pulling them quickly into the house.

After Feng Shui enhancements were completed, prospective buyers no longer paused at the negative view and began spending more time in the house appreciating its strong selling points. After the next open house, an offer was accepted and the sellers were able to move on to new job opportunities out of the area.

Use a Bagua mirror to deflect unwanted energy.

What to Do When There's No Traffic / No Offers

If no one is coming to see the home, the energy of buyers is stagnant, and you have to get things moving in the Buyer area of the house and property.

Hang a wind chime both inside the house in the near right corner, and outside under the eaves of the house in the near right corner. If the "For Sale" sign is not already placed there, move it to the near right corner of the lot by the street. Add streamers or balloons for extra movement. Call those buyers in!

Double-check that the near right side of the home is not a bathroom. If it is, go earthy in this room to stop draining the Buyer energy. Add towels and décor in earth tones, and be sure the toilet seat is down and drains are closed. Place a small pot of bamboo in the bathroom, perhaps on the toilet tank, to help lift this energy.

Another important factor in the case of no traffic is to reevaluate the photos you are using of the property. Be sure the front door is clearly visible in at least one of the photos. This increases the welcome factor and makes the house more approachable. Make sure that your photos do not show the backs of couches or chairs. This makes the room you are photographing look smaller and is very off-putting. Include photos depicting the selling points of the house, e.g., great view of golf course, large family room, or gourmet kitchen.

Get the Seller to Let Go

It can be a common experience that if the seller is ambivalent about selling the home, it is much harder to sell. When the seller is holding on, the buyer has to energetically push his way into the house and often feels like an unwelcome trespasser. Getting the seller to release the property can often be the final straw that sells the house.

Giving the seller something physical to do to release the house is a sure-fire way to bring all hesitation to the forefront to be dissolved. Here's one technique we have had much success with:

Have the seller chip three small pieces off the foundation of the house. Easy places to access this are usually in the garage, in the basement, or around the back of the house. A hammer and a screwdriver are all that is needed to accomplish this. (We're talking small symbolic pieces, not huge chunks of concrete!)

Next, the seller takes these pieces to flowing water. A favorite hike with a stream, a lake, a waterfall in a park, even an irrigation ditch will do. The seller throws the pieces of house foundation in the direction of the water flowing away and waves goodbye. The idea is that the seller is letting go of the house so that buyers may more easily claim it for themselves.

Have the seller pay attention to any feelings or emotions that surface at this time. They may be angry, resentful, sad—whatever comes up, now is the time to experience it and release it. It is often surprising to find out that they were not dealing with feelings associated with selling the house. This truly can be one of the last barriers to go before the property sells.

Last, but not least, they should picture what the sale of the house looks like to them. This is very subjective, but it might be a "SOLD" sign, or receiving a check from you, or the moving van pulling up in the driveway. No matter what the mental picture, it will seed the intention energetically for the sale of the house.

The backup plan is to do this yourself. But *only* if the seller is really resistant to performing this releasing ceremony should you step in and help things along by doing it for them.

Success Story

The stories of clients letting go of a house and it selling within the week, or even the day, are legion. One that stands out is that of a cowboy, recently widowed, who was ready to sell "this broken down old place" (actually, a very nice ranch). After the property had been staged, which included a barn he had built himself, it did not sell quickly. After a few weeks, it was suggested that perhaps a release of the property was in order, even though the seller indicated he was more than ready to go.

Foundation pieces were chipped from the ranch house and from the barn and taken down to where a small stream runs through and away from the property. The seller threw his foundation pieces in the stream and immediately broke down in tears. Prior to this moment, he had not come to terms with all that the property, and his life together with his wife there, meant to him. Needless to say, it helped him to release the house and allowed someone else to easily buy it, above asking price, within the next few weeks.

SELL YOUR HOME WITH FENG SHUI

Chapter 9

Chapter 9

LISTEN TO BUYERS' COMMENTS

Getting feedback from your showings and those of other agents is essential. You need to know specifically why a potential buyer did not make an offer. Often, the same issues with the house keep coming up. If you find that a particular aspect of the house is holding off a sale, you can address it with Feng Shui.

Rooms are Too Small—Change Perception

If a chronic complaint is that a particular room is too small, there are several enhancements to change this perception. Painting one or two accent walls in smaller rooms can remove the boxy feeling and give the room more dimension. If the far wall can be the accent wall, this is a plus. It really pulls the buyer into the room by giving it a bit of drama and depth.

You can increase the size of a great room by shifting furniture that divides the room, such as long couches. If the room is broken into two or more seating or living areas, combine them into one for your showings. The first impression of the space will be much larger. Remember, we are staging for the buyer rather than the comfort of the seller.

Using fewer, larger pieces of artwork can also enlarge the room. Several small or disparate pieces tend to fragment the space and make it appear smaller. Raise valances up above the tops of windows, or remove them entirely. This way the windows look larger, allow more light inside, and create a feeling of more space.

Add depth to a room with an accent wall.

Up the lighting quotient. Use "daylight" bulbs to brighten up and expand the feeling in a room. Also, be sure to thin out the furniture if needed and keep only the pieces that are proportional and appropriate to each room.

Too Many Stairs—Moderate Impact

You can moderate the impact of too many stairs in a number of ways. One is to place a strong piece of art at the top. This gives the eye a destination and helps to pull the buyer up the stairs. Make sure the stairwell has good lighting. A long, dark stairwell is very uninviting.

Remove any blocking furniture or decorative objects in stairwells. You want the stairs to appear as wide as possible. The only décor a stairwell needs is light and color. If you hang more than one piece of art in the stairwell, it can emphasize the steepness of the stairs with a "stair-step" effect. Art hung on both walls of a stairwell tends to cramp and narrow the path. Therefore, light, bright, and open is the way to go with stairs.

Too Much Street Noise—Downplay with Diversion

You can't change the street, but you can change the effect of street noise on the buyer. Determine where the greatest impact of street noise is inside the house. Wherever that might be is the place to create a diversion for the ear of the buyer.

Hang a wind chime outside this window, one that has a nice harmonious sound. This creates a foreground sound and pushes the street noise to the background. The same can be done by adding a small water fountain to a room dominated by outside noise. Another solution is to have soft music playing when the house is shown.

Given an alternative, the ear will always go to the more charming sound in the environment first. So give the buyer a choice and create a sonic diversion.

SELL YOUR HOME WITH FENG SHUI

Chapter 10

Chapter 10

SELL AN EMPTY HOUSE

An empty house can be easily staged for a quick sale. With just a few items, the house can often be shown to its greatest advantage. Sometimes less is more, especially if the house was previously filled with furniture, photos, children's toys, and other clutter. The space and dimensions of the house are now visible, and you can enhance the Feng Shui strong points.

Set Up a Vignette

You want to create a place for the buyer to sit down and think about making an offer on the house. The best way to accomplish this is to set up a vignette with a small table and chairs. This will avoid the usual "quick walk through the house and then out the door into the car" pattern. After such a visit, the buyer then has to remember the house from a distance. Rarely can a buyer take away with them how it felt in the house and what particularly appealed to them.

Instead, when you give the buyer a place to pause, sit, and discuss the house, it reinforces the welcoming feeling of the house and the strong selling points. The best place for this vignette is in the Buyer area of the house. This strengthens the *chi* of purchasing the house. The exception to this is if the Buyer *gua* turns out to be the bathroom, the garage, the laundry room, or some other less desirable room.

If that is the case, then simply set up the vignette in the best room in the house. Perhaps it is the great room, or next to a window with the best view, or in a fabulous master suite, or where they can see through to several rooms at once.

The location will be your subjective call, and it is a very important decision. This is the room that will help to sell the house. It is the room where the buyer will pause, spend a little extra time, and decide that this is the house for them!

A word about the vignette furniture: Dress up the table with a nice cloth. Use chairs that have arms and backs. Nice chairs let the buyer relax and feel taken care of. (Much better than armless folding chairs or stools.) The table does not have to be large, but it should have at least three chairs. Put a vertical holder with the house flyers on the table. This is another incentive to pull the buyer over to this special sales spot.

The small effort required to create this vignette in a vacant listing will pay off with an easier sale. You can, of course, recycle this vignette to your next vacant home on the inventory.

Success Story

Listing agents of a small, older home in a cul-de-sac that had been on the market the year before and now again, with no offer, decided to try staging with Feng Shui. The house was empty and the sellers were not motivated to put any money into fixing up this much abused rental. There was only one nice room in the house and this was the kitchen. It was decided to place the vignette in the kitchen, so that a buyer would pause here and appreciate the charm of this room. There were pleasant views out both kitchen windows, one a mountain in the distance and the other a small garden area. The window coverings were lifted up to expose these views.

The vignette consisted of a nice table and three chairs, covered with a bright cloth matching the decorative tile of the kitchen. A standing container for house flyers was also placed here to draw the buyer over to the table. An offer on this house came in the same week, without the seller doing the painting, carpeting, and other upgrades the house needed.

A vignette creates a place for the buyer to sit down and think about making an offer.

Enhance Curb Appeal

Making the mouth of chi/front door welcoming is even more important when it comes to staging a vacant house. Use all your Feng Shui techniques from Chapter 2. Here's a quick review:

Clear the path to the front door so that it is wide and inviting. If possible, add another stepping-stone path directly from the street to the entrance to bring the *chi* and the buyer straight up to the door.

Make locating the house as easy as possible by using large, readable house numbers on a contrasting background. Provide a fresh front-door mat, as large as the opening. Use a double-size mat for a double-door entry.

The front door needs to be visible and welcoming. Give it a fresh coat of paint or stain so that it pops! And don't forget that the "For Sale" sign is best placed in the front right corner of the lot, the Buyer's area.

None of these suggestions requires maintenance by the seller or yourself. Once they are set in place, they can assist an empty house to sell.

Flowers on an entry path enlivens an empty house.

73

Emphasize the Room of First Impression

The principle of emphasis on the room of first impression still holds true in an empty house. Pick the best room, the one that will sell the house. Lay down a path to the room of first impression with a runner rug. Or hang a single piece of art or a mirror on the wall in the direction you want the buyer to go.

If this is truly the best room in the house, then you may place your vignette of furniture here to provide a place for the buyer to sit and appreciate the house from this vantage point.

Energize the Buyer Area

Don't forget this important area for Feng Shui enhancement. This is the place to charge up the energy to bring the buyer in, even in an uninhabited house.

Use wind chimes to call in the buyer in the right front corner of the house, up under the eaves outside. In the right front corner on the inside of the house, you can use another chime or a round, faceted crystal to enliven the energy for buyers.

This is also an area to place a flag on the house, especially if the house sits in a cul-de-sac. If the front right section of the house is missing, such as in an L-shaped house, then complete the missing *gua* by placing large rocks, a birdbath, or a tree at the missing intersection—that is, where the two walls of the house would have met had the house been squared off.

Use Paint to Enliven a Room

As you are well aware from your real estate experience, painting can always make a house look and feel fresh and clean.

Our Feng Shui tip in this regard is to use the paint where it will do the most good. Paint accent walls in small, boxy rooms to open them up. Use a light, bright trim color on the house to make it feel larger and give it a lift for curb appeal. Paint the front door a contrasting, brighter, or deeper tone than the trim and body of the house.

If the seller is willing to commit to painting, then make it really work to sell the house as quickly and easily as possible.

Bring life to the Buyer area with a waving flag.

SELL YOUR HOME WITH FENG SHUI

Chapter 11

Chapter 11

PREPARE YOUR FENG SHUI STAGING KIT

We suggest that you prepare and keep a box or basket in the trunk of your car with Feng Shui staging materials packed and ready for use in any staging and selling situation that may come up. Create your own kit with containers that are easy to use.

Be sure to stock multiples of those items you find you use most frequently.

- Metal dish with business cards

- Standing plastic holder for flyers

- For Sale sign

- Wind chimes with hollow metal tubes

- Bagua Mirror

- Round, faceted crystal

- Red candles

- Runner rug

- Two pots with red silk flowers

- Welcome mats
  (for single and double doors)

- Copies of *Sell Your Home With Feng Shui*
  for your sellers.

Also, keep the following items handy:

- Vignette furniture: small table, 3 or 4 chairs with arms, nice tablecloth

- Small desktop fountain

- Pot of bamboo

Produce Effective Promotional Photos

Your photos for the Internet, flyers, virtual tours, and other promotional materials need to tie in with your Feng Shui staging for best results. A picture of the room of first impression is essential. If the view, the great master suite, or the unique fireplace are selling points, then, of course, these are photos that need to be included as well.

When the buyer arrives to view the property and the expectations created by the photos are satisfied, they will immediately feel at home and more inclined to buy.

Another Feng Shui tip: When taking an outside photo of the house, be sure that the front door is visible. This is another energetic way to give the buyer a welcome and send the message that the house is accessible and available.

Keep your Feng Shui Staging Kit ready to go.

SELL YOUR HOME WITH FENG SHUI

Chapter 12

Chapter 12

INCREASE SALES
WITH FENG SHUI STAGING

The ancient technique of Feng Shui has proven itself as a modern tool for real estate sales. Join thousands of other real estate professionals and homeowners who have reaped the benefits of using Feng Shui in real estate staging. Houses that sit stagnant on the market literally take on new life when Feng Shui solutions are brought to bear. Interest in your listings and increased showings are commonplace. Offers come in promptly and obstacles to a quick sale seem to dissolve.

You will find that after using Feng Shui to stage your listings and experiencing the boost in your sales, it will be a natural addition to your marketing regime. It is easy to incorporate the suggestions in this book without investing a lot of time and money. Feng Shui enhancements can be made quickly and often with objects at hand. These techniques will give you a definite edge in moving your inventory.

No matter how long you have been involved in real estate, you now have a new Feng Shui sensibility for how a house can welcome and bring in a buyer. You will approach the staging process at a deeper, more powerful level.

You can give your seller a copy of *Sell Your Home With Feng Shui* to help them understand what you are doing and why. It will help them be a positive team member and often generates extra excitement in the staging process. Instead of feeling inconvenienced, sellers often want to help in a Feng Shui way!

In the rare exception of a listing that refuses to move even after all of your best staging efforts, you may need additional assistance. Call in a Feng Shui professional to do work of a more transcendental nature. A trained Feng Shui consultant can address the energy of a home on a very deep level. It requires specialized training and experience and cannot be conveyed properly in the context of a book.

This might be the case if real trauma has occurred in connection with the house, e.g., death, burglary, assault, or long-term illness. Both energetic cleansing and releasing of the house can be accomplished for you by a professional.

The best way to find your local Feng Shui expert is by referral. Ask around and find the person with the best reputation for results.

Quick Reference Guide
to Sell Your Home with Feng Shui

CURB APPEAL

__For Sale signage in right front corner.

__Unobstructed path to front door.

__Large readable house numbers on house and mailbox.

__Welcome bench on porch, if space permits.

__No cracked concrete or stepping stones.

FRONT DOORS

__Dramatic front door, enhanced with color and new hardware.

__Easily opened front door.

__Matching pots of bright flowers or foliage framing door.

__Welcome mat as wide as door.

__Hidden front door (see Chapter2).

BELOW GRADE HOMES

__Lights, house numbers, or decoration set high on façade.

__Trim painted a bright, light color.

__Weathervane on peak of roof.

OUTSIDE STAIRS

__Welcome mat at base of stairs.

__Matching pots of flowers or foliage at base of stairs.

__Benches or flowers on landings, if space permits.

__Welcoming statuary.

ENTRY/FOYER

__*Table with real estate business cards in metal dish.*

__*Good lighting.*

__*Art that reinforces selling point of home or large mirror.*

__*Direct buyer to selected room of first impression.*

__*No blocking furniture.*

ROOM OF FIRST IMPRESSION

__*Welcoming furniture arrangement.*

__*One large seating area.*

__*Unobstructed pathway to views.*

__*Accent wall to enlarge room.*

__*Mirror or art in reflective glass to bring any view into room.*

BEDROOMS

__*No desks or exercise equipment.*

__*Properly proportioned bedroom furniture.*

__*Bed placed on far wall.*

__*Accent bed wall with color.*

INSIDE STAIRS

__*Art at top of stairs.*

__*Well lit.*

__*If two staircases at entry, direct to room of first impression.*

__*No furniture or stair-stepped art inside stairwell.*

START PACKING

__*Personal items and family photos.*

__*Collections.*

__*Any potentially offensive items.*

__*Clutter.*

CAREER GUA (FRONT AND CENTER)

__*Water element: fountain, fish, art with water depicted.*

__*Business cards in metal dish.*

BUYER GUA (FRONT RIGHT)

__*Metal wind chimes with hollow tubes.*

__*Flag at right angle to street.*

__*For Sale signage.*

__*If necessary, complete missing gua with boulder or tree.*

FAME GUA (REAR CENTER)

__*Red items: candles, flowers, art.*

__*Barbeque, fire pit, fireplace.*

__*Logs in fireplace.*

WEALTH GUA (FAR LEFT)

__*Water element (as in Career Gua above).*

__*Items in purple, red, green, silver, or gold.*

__*Expensive items.*

__*Metal wind chimes.*

UNIVERSAL CURES (IN ANY GUA)
__*Round, faceted crystal.*
__*Pot of bamboo.*
__*Bagua Mirror facing any offending view.*

STAGING EMPTY HOUSE
__*Vignette with table and chairs.*
__*Enhanced curb appeal (see above).*
__*Staged room of first impression (see above).*
__*Energized Buyer Gua (see above).*

PROMOTIONAL PHOTOS
__*Front door.*
__*Selling points: view, master suite, gourmet kitchen.*
__*Room of first impression.*

HOUSE WITH BAD REPUTATION
__*Enhance Fame Gua (see above).*
__*Give property a new name.*

NEGATIVE/DOMINANT ADJACENT PROPERTY
__*Weathervane on peak of roof.*
__*Bagua Mirror to block offending views.*
__*Screen with trees or shrubs.*

NO TRAFFIC / NO OFFERS
__*Enhance Buyer Gua (see above).*
__*New promotional photos (see above).*

Getting Seller to Let Go

__Packing (see above).

__Releasing ceremony (see Chapter 8).

Rooms Are Too Small

__Accent walls.

__Less furniture and art.

__Raise or remove window valances.

__Good lighting.

Street Noise

__Wind chimes

__Water fountain.

__Soft music.

Feng Shui Staging Kit

(See Chapter 11.)

Acknowledgements

The authors wish to thank the following real estate professionals, clients, family, and friends for their assistance in manifesting this book:

Lynn Avery, Robert Ayres, Nancy Barton, Diane Brown, Jay and Robyn Champlain, Shari Chase, David and Jasper Coverdale, Patti Davidson, Emily DeHuff, Kelly Elcano, Patty Eikam, Pam Fernandez, Byron and Jasna Gehring, Margo Groth, Marne Humphries, Jason and Danielle Kirby, Pat Lear, Richard Leviton, Shahri and David Masters, Beverly McKenney, Cathy Nason, Norm Nicholls, Anna Grahn-Nilsson, Ann Nguyen, Debbie and Richard Poudrier, Mary Reimer, Schaller Family, Diane and Bill Simmons, Joy Strotz, Cheri and Tom Taranowski, Ann Marie Trowbridge, and Trinkie Watson.

About the Authors

Christine Ayres is a professional Feng Shui consultant who has been involved with Feng Shui since 1989. She lived, worked, and studied in Hong Kong for four years. Her company, Feng Shui Services, is based in the Lake Tahoe area of California and Nevada. She has appeared on radio and television both here and abroad. Her work has been recognized by the national *Feng Shui Journal* and she has published regular columns on Feng Shui over the past ten years. She is married to astrologer Robert Ayres. Contact her at aalchemy@sbcglobal.net

Cindy Coverdale, certified Feng Shui consultant, began her studies in transcendental energy in 1999. She continues to expand her knowledge of Feng Shui as a member of the Katherine Metz Affiliate Program, studying the Black Sect teachings of Professor Lin Yun Rinpoche. She lives in the Lake Tahoe area with her husband, musician David Coverdale, and their son. She previously co-authored *Food That Rocks*, available from Conari Press. Visit her website, EnergeticArtistry.com.

To contact the authors regarding Staging Real Estate with Feng Shui presentations or services:

www.sellyourhomewithfengshui.com.

3534853

Made in the USA